American Composers of the 20th Century

23 Piano Pieces for the Student Pianist

ISBN: 978-1-4234-2500-7

EDWARD B. MARKS MUSIC COMPANY

EXCLUSIVELY DISTRIBUTED BY

HAL•LEONARD® CORPORATION

7777 W. BLUEMOUND RD. P.O. BOX 13819 MILWAUKEE, WI 53213

Visit Hal Leonard Online at
www.halleonard.com

CONTENTS

Milton Babbitt
Duet 1

Arthur Berger
Intermezzo 2

Sol Berkowitz
March of the Puppets 4

Mario Castelnuovo-Tedesco
Prelude 9

Norman Cazden
Game 6

Henry Cowell
Toccatina 8

Norman Dello Joio
Night Song 12

Vivian Fine
The Small Sad Sparrow 14

Miriam Gideon
Walk 15

Lou Harrison
Little Suite for Piano
    Pastoral 16
    Quadrille 17
    Chorale 18

Robert Helps
Starscape 20

Alan Hovhaness
Lullaby 19

Jan Meyerowitz
Noel Far from Home 22

Charles Mills
A Child's Daydream 24

Hall Overton
A Mood 25

Joseph Prostakoff
Parade 26

Karol Rathaus
Echo 27

Roger Sessions
Little Piece 30
Waltz for Brenda 28

Nicolas Slonimsky
Pastoral 31

Robert Starer
"Above, Below and Between" 32

William Sydeman
Prelude 35

Ben Weber
Lyric Piece 36

BIOGRAPHICAL SKETCHES

Milton Babbitt
born 1916 in Philadelphia, grew up in Jackson, Mississippi; studied at Princeton, where he now teaches [2009] as well as at Juilliard; co-founded Columbia-Princeton Electronic Music Studio; received lifetime Pulitzer Prize in 1982.

Arthur Berger
born 1912 in New York City; pupil of Piston, Milhaud and Boulanger; taught at Mills College, Brandeis University and New England Conservatory; music critic from 1943-46; died 2003 in Boston.

Sol Berkowitz
born 1922 in Warren, Ohio; studied with Luening and Rathaus; longtime professor at Queens College; composed for all mediums including Broadway, film and television; author of several widely used textbooks on ear training; died 2006 in New York.

Mario Castelnuovo-Tedesco
born 1895 in Florence, Italy; studied with Pizzetti; to U. S. in 1939; composed film scores for MGM in Hollywood and for all mediums including opera; died 1968 in Beverly Hills, California.

Norman Cazden
born 1914 in New York City; studied with Wagenaar, Piston and Copland; taught at Vassar, Peabody, Universities of Michigan and Illinois and The New School; researched American folk music; died 1980 in Bangor, Maine.

Henry Cowell
born 1897 in Menlo Park, California; largely self-taught with some studies at the University of California and in New York; highly individual composer who created or explored many innovative techniques such as polytonality, polyrhythm, clusters and aleatoric music, often for the piano; his book "New Musical Resources" influenced Cage, Nancarrow and countless others; died 1965 in Shady, New York.

Norman Dello Joio
born 1913 in New York; studied with his organist father, later with Wagenaar and Hindemith; taught at Sarah Lawrence, Mannes and Boston University; directed the Ford Foundation Contemporary Music Project from 1959-73; winner of the 1957 Pulitzer Prize in music; composer of many works for every medium; died 2008 in East Hampton, New York.

Vivian Fine
born 1913 in Chicago; studied with Ruth Crawford and Roger Sessions; co-founded American Composers' Alliance; taught at New York University, Juilliard and Bennington College; died 2000 in Bennington, Vermont.

Miriam Gideon

born 1906 in Greely, Colorado; studied with Lazare Saminsky and Roger Sessions; taught at Brooklyn College, Manhattan School of Music, and City College of New York; died 1996 in New York City.

Lou Harrison

born 1917 in Portland, Oregon; studied with Cowell and Schoenberg; taught at Mills College, UCLA and Black Mountain College; also active as a conductor, instrument maker, inventor, constructor of mobiles and florist; died 2003 in Lafayette, Indiana.

Robert Helps

born 1928 in Passaic, New Jersey; studied piano with Abby Whiteside and composition with Roger Sessions; a virtuoso pianist, taught piano at Princeton, New England Conservatory, and Stanford among others, and music at the University of South Florida; died 2001 in Tampa, Florida.

Alan Hovhaness

born 1911 in Somerville, Massachusetts; studied with Frederick Converse and Bohuslav Martinů; highly prolific composer influenced by a variety of world music, particularly of Asia and Armenia; died 2000 in Seattle.

Jan Meyerowitz

born 1913 in Breslau, Germany (now Wroclaw, Poland); studied with Zemlinsky, Respighi and Casella; to U. S. in 1946; taught at Brooklyn College and City College of New York in the 1960's and 70's; died 1998 in Colmar, France.

Charles Mills

born 1914 in Asheville, North Carolina; studied with Max Garfield, Aaron Copland, Roger Sessions and Roy Harris; composed orchestral and film music; taught at Manhattan School of Music; died 1982.

Hall Overton

born 1920 in Bangor, Michigan; studied with Persichetti, Riegger and Milhaud; extensive experience in jazz; taught at Yale and Juilliard; arranged for Thelonious Monk; died 1972 in New York City.

Joseph Prostakoff

born 1911 in Central Asia; studied piano with Abby Whiteside and composition with Rathaus; taught piano and worked as piano music editor in New York City; died 1980.

Karol Rathaus

born 1895 in Tarnopol, Poland; studied with Franz Schreker in Vienna; to U. S. in 1938; taught at Queens College; composed music for all mediums including film; died 1954 in New York.

Roger Sessions

born 1896 in Brooklyn, New York; studied with Horatio Parker and Ernest Bloch; taught at Princeton and Juilliard among others; winner of the 1982 Pulitzer Prize in music and many other prizes; died 1985 in Princeton, New Jersey.

Nicolas Slonimsky

born 1894 in St. Petersburg, Russia; to U. S. in 1923; known primarily as a writer, though played piano, coached opera and conducted several important premieres; composed piano pieces and commercial jingles; died 1995 in Los Angeles.

Robert Starer

born 1924 in Vienna, Austria; studied in Jerusalem; to U. S. in 1947 and studied with Copland; taught at Juilliard; works for all mediums including operas and ballets; died 2001 in Kingston, New York.

William Sydeman

born 1928 in New York City; studied at Mannes College with Sessions, later taught there; prolific output for all mediums; underwent a stylistic change in 1980 after a pause from composing; currently lives in Nevada City, California [2009].

Ben Weber

born 1916 in St. Louis; largely self-taught; moved to New York in 1945; worked as music copyist and restauranteur; composed many chamber music works, piano, songs; died 1979 in New York City.

FOREWORD FROM THE ORIGINAL PUBLICATION

Great care has been taken to select music for this volume that is fundamentally easy to play. Nevertheless, the pieces differ not only in style but also somewhat in grade of difficulty. This is caused by the very nature of the contemporary scene, where influences from all directions are making themselves felt, from the traditional to the revolutionary, the emotional to the intellectual, the compliant to the defiant and all cross relations thereof. Contemporary music is a reflection of the times as was the music of the past. It is not a dead conglomerate of school forms but a fascinating, live near-chaos out of which the succeeding era is forming. Only the past is clear.

It would not serve the student's purposes to give him dry, theoretical explanations. Much of this music defies commentary anyway since it is too new and too fresh to be subjected to such procedures. Moreover, the mechanical knowledge, i.e. whether a twelve-tone melody is built on the basic row or on the inversion of it, does not disclose its musical nature and value. Only intensive occupation with the music itself will open the door to understanding; only then, as by intuition, will we become aware of how to play a certain phrase or line, or how to emphasize an important harmony. Progressing from there, we will begin to comprehend the entire work.

It is not possible to put normal gradings of difficulty on the various compositions. Sometimes problems will be encountered not for technical reasons but because of insufficient comprehension of the music. Frequently, such problems are psychological and disappear on closer penetration of the content. It is, therefore, advisable, just as with any other music, to first select for study the pieces that appeal most on first acquaintance and then to proceed to the seemingly more difficult to understand. The result of this method will be surprising to the student. He will find that the differences in style and degree of difficulty are not nearly so great as he initially thought them to be. He will become aware that the music of today can be enjoyed just as much as that of the past.

FOREWORD TO THE PRESENT EDITION

Since the year of its first publication, 1956, this collection of piano pieces has become a staple of a piano (and music appreciation) pedagogy which strives to bring the intermediate student into contact with contemporary music. Its disappearance from publication in recent decades has been answered by a collective outcry for its re-publication. Though the piano pieces are no longer "contemporary" by definition, the collection's enduring popularity reveals its positive impact as a teaching tool. What, then, does it teach?

This book succeeds in its aim to capture compositional styles of the mid-20th century while channeling the voices of some of America's favorite and most dedicated composers for the purpose of music education (and fun). In very few places can we find some of these composers welcoming young hands and ears into sound worlds essential to the 20th century. Young musicians are introduced to the harmonic languages of atonality, unique uses of tonality, and worlds in between by leading pioneers of the century. This collection teaches us that musical (or artistic) style does not live and die, rather it is born and lives forever, fusing with styles that have come before, occasionally being imitated anew, sometimes causing an opposite stylistic reaction that is in itself evidence of its vitality.

Perhaps the very best reason for bringing this particular book back into publication is that there is simply nothing else like it. The editors have retained nearly everything of the 1956 edition. The only alteration is to the list of composer biographies, which have been updated in the most minimal fashion possible.

for Betty Ann

Duet

MILTON BABBITT

Intermezzo

ARTHUR BERGER

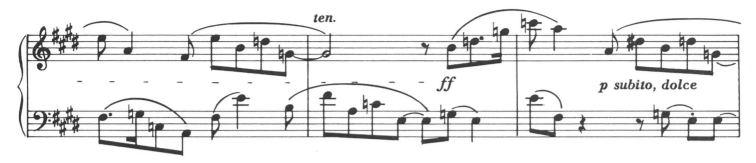

1948

*) Depress pedal just after key is released.

March of the Puppets

SOL BERKOWITZ

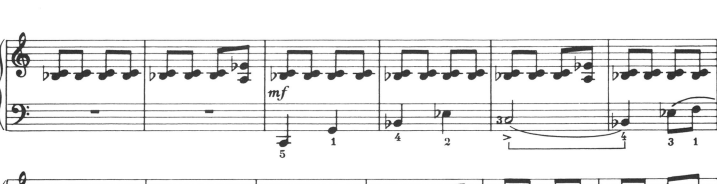

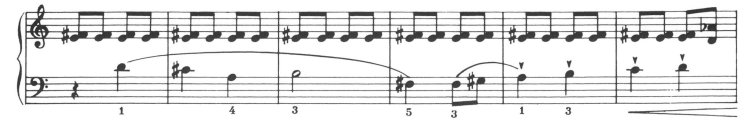

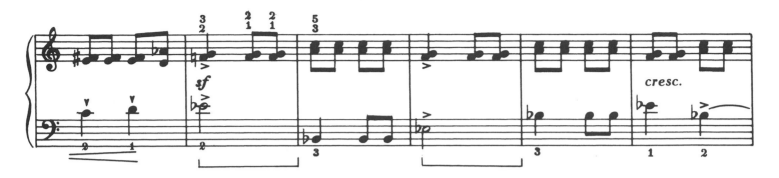

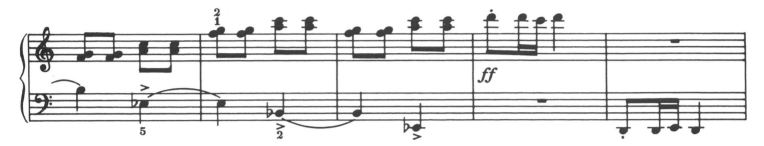

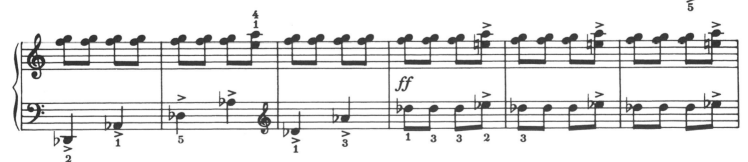

Game

NORMAN CAZDEN

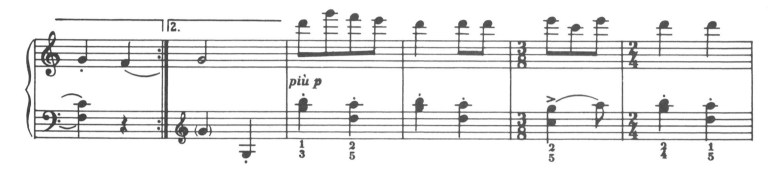

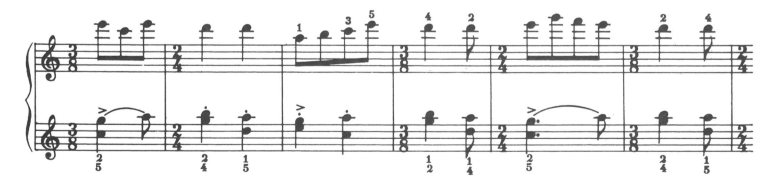

Toccatina

HENRY COWELL

Prelude

MARIO CASTELNUOVO-TEDESCO

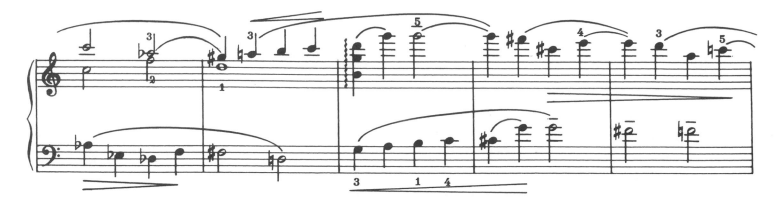

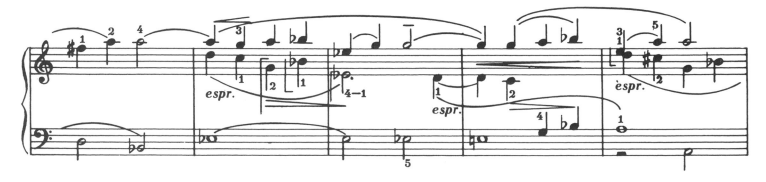

11

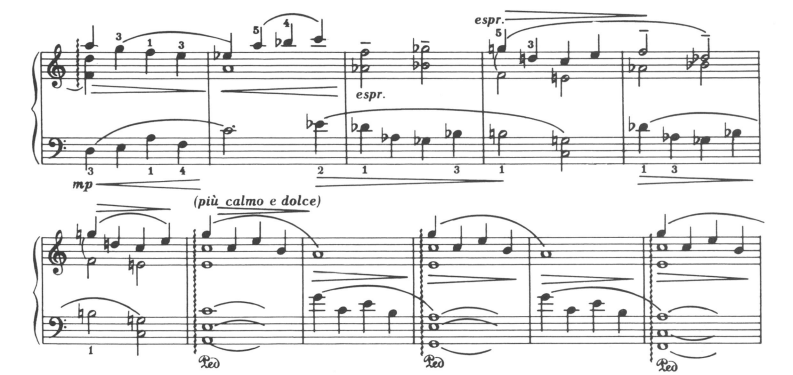

Tempo I *(calmo e dolce)*

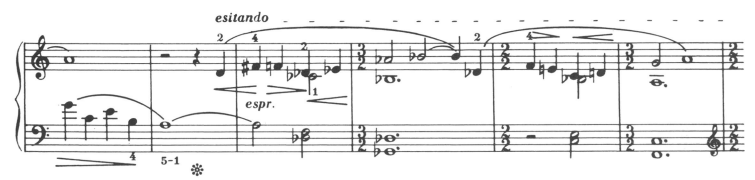

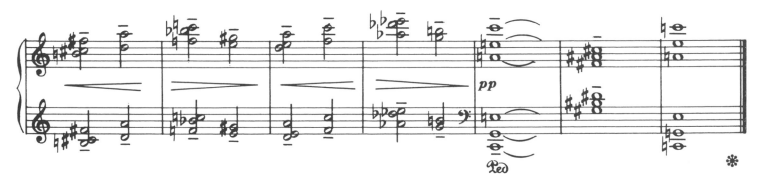

Night Song

NORMAN DELLO JOIO

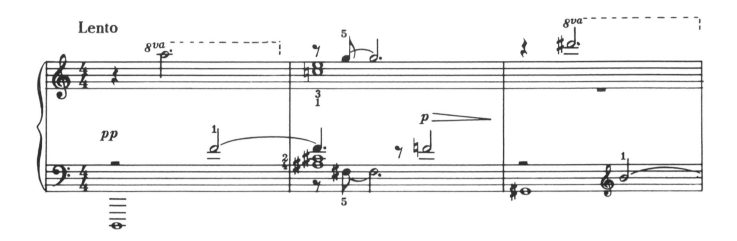

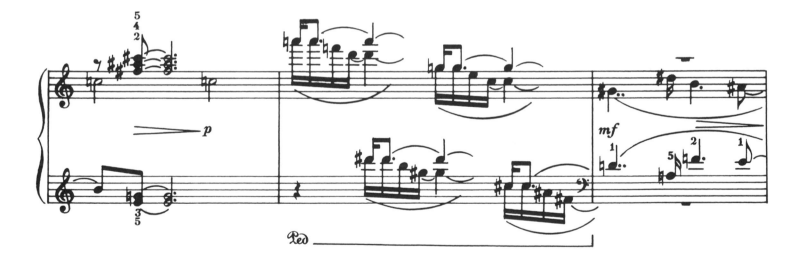

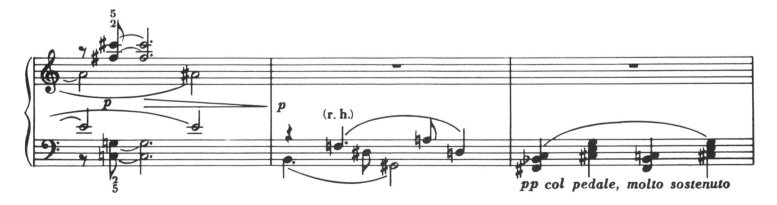

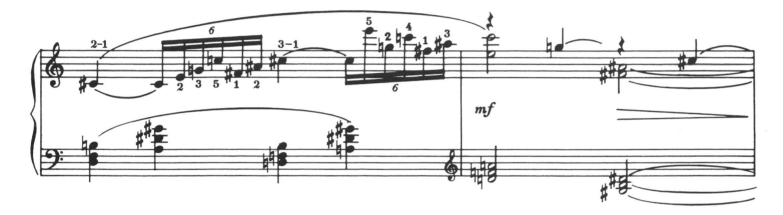

The Small Sad Sparrow

VIVIAN FINE

Walk
(Thirds)

MIRIAM GIDEON

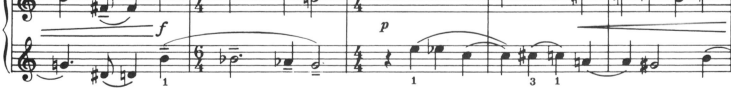

Little Suite for Piano
Pastorale

LOU HARRISON

Quadrille

17

Chorale

Lullaby

ALAN HOVHANESS

Starscape

ROBERT HELPS

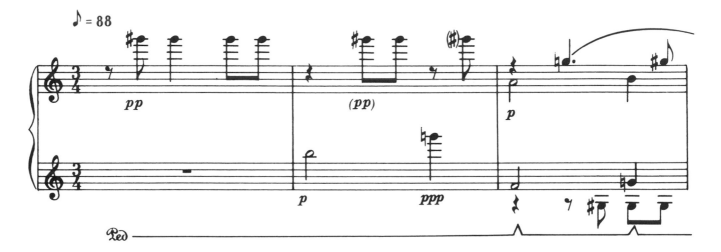

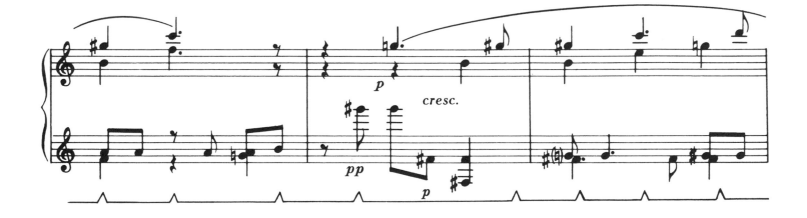

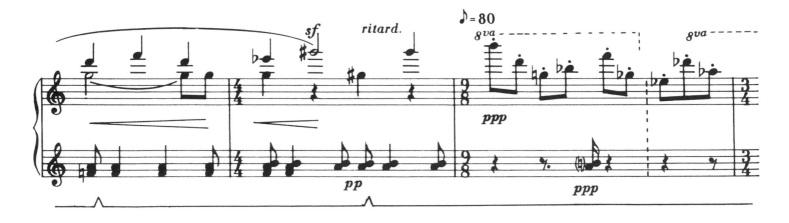

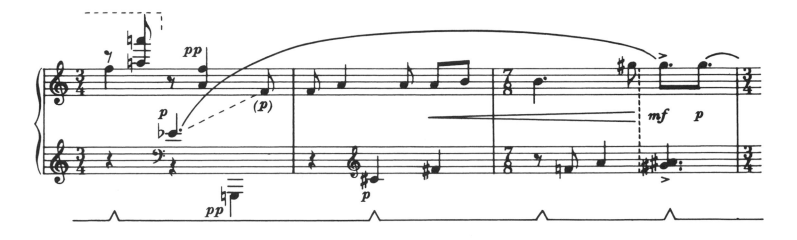

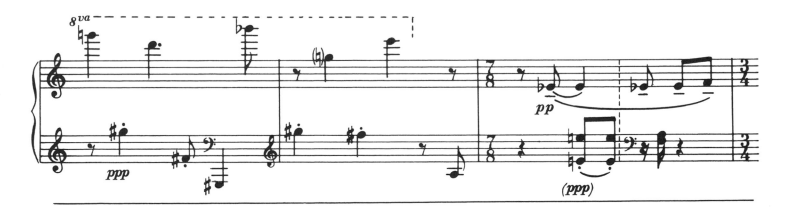

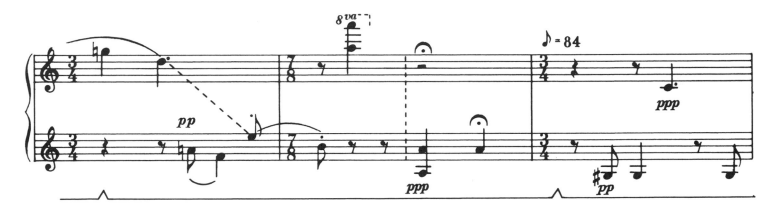

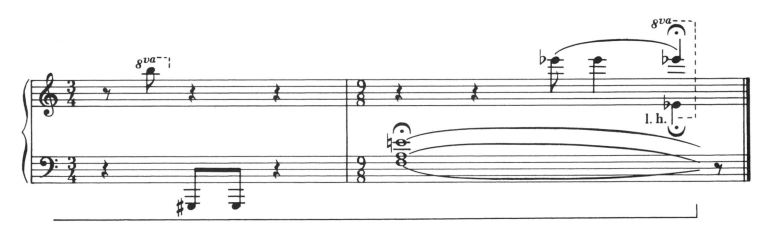

to Caterina D' Amico

Noel Far from Home

JAN MEYEROWITZ

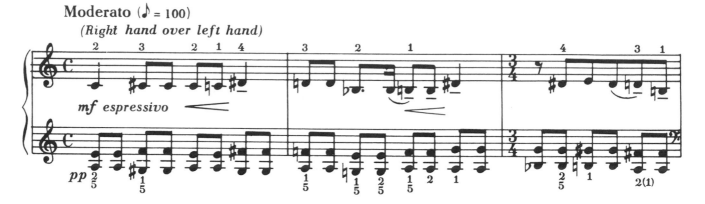

*) *The eighth - note maintains the same value throughout.*

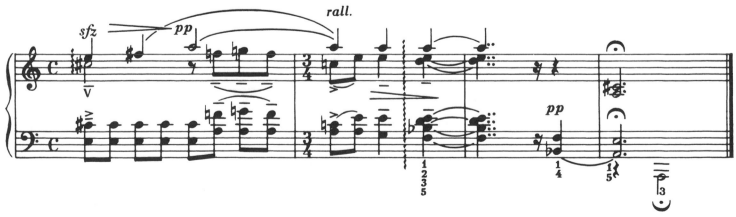

to Sheilah Anne Mills

A Child's Daydream

CHARLES MILLS

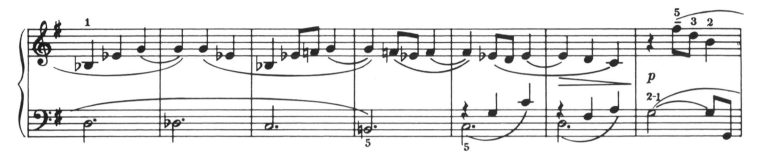

A Mood

HALL OVERTON

Parade

JOSEPH PROSTAKOFF

Echo

KAROL RATHAUS

Waltz for Brenda

ROGER SESSIONS

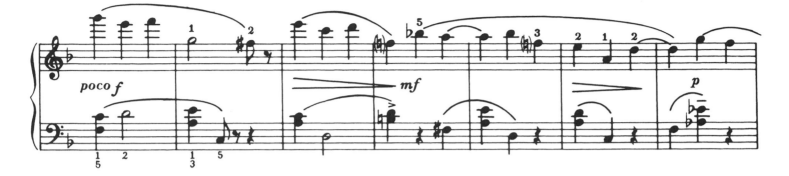

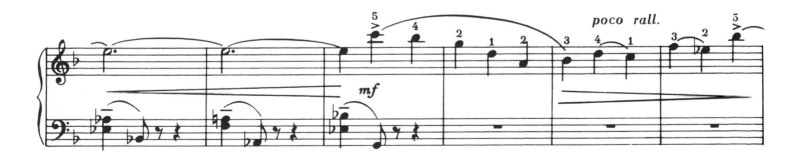

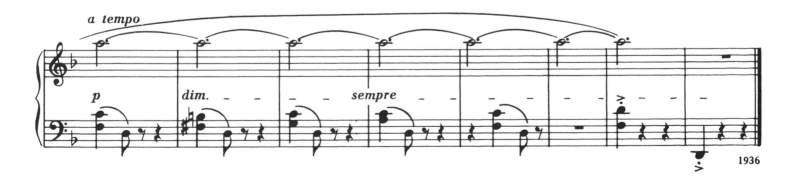

1936

for John, age 1

Little Piece

ROGER SESSIONS

1939

Pastoral

NICOLAS SLONIMSKY

"Above, Below and Between"

ROBERT STARER

below and between

above

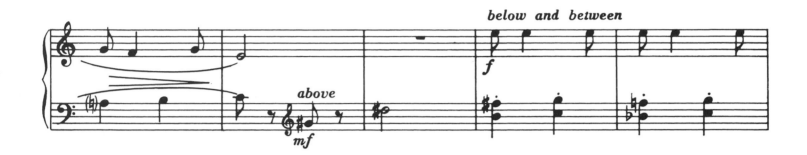

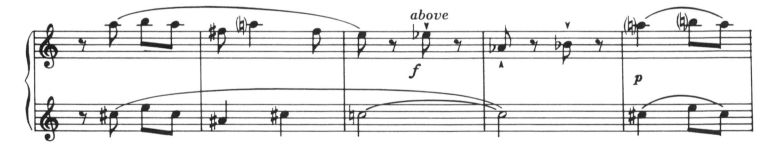

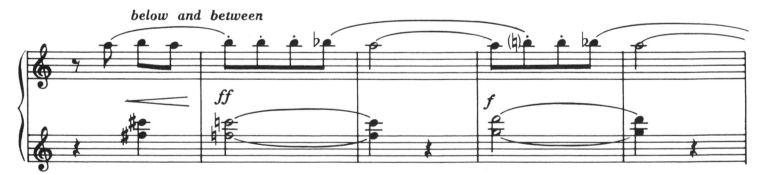

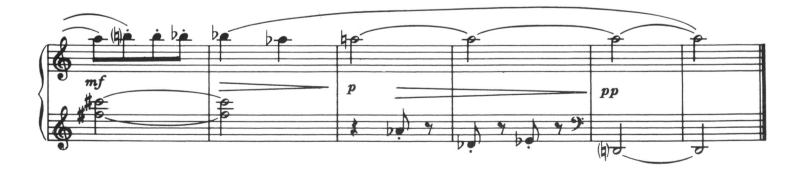

Prelude

WILLIAM SYDEMAN

*) ├──→ *indicates "accel." over length of arrow, followed by "a tempo".*

Lyric Piece

BEN WEBER
Op. 40a

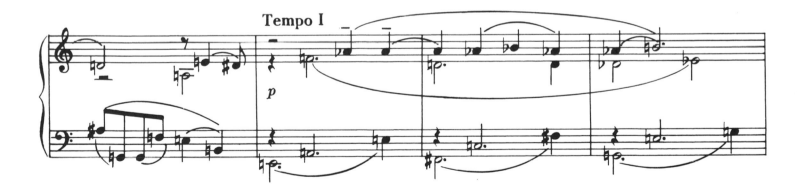

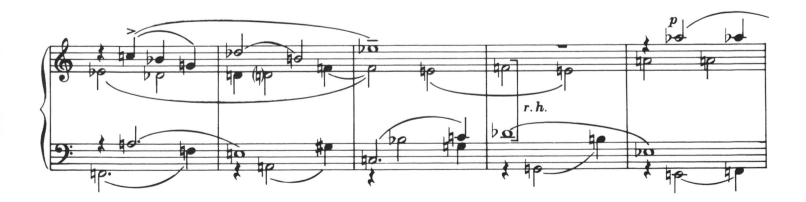

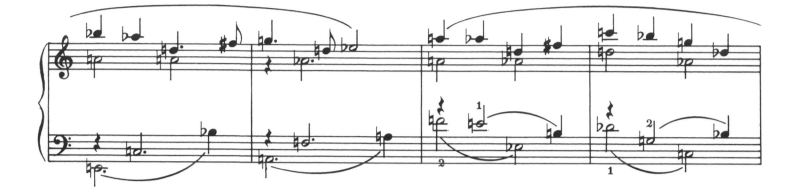

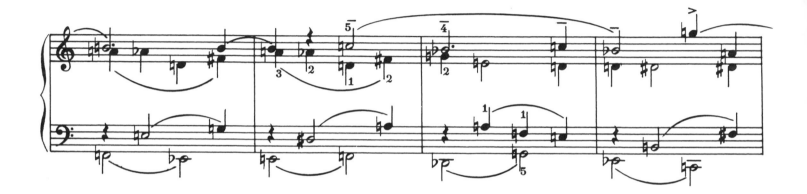

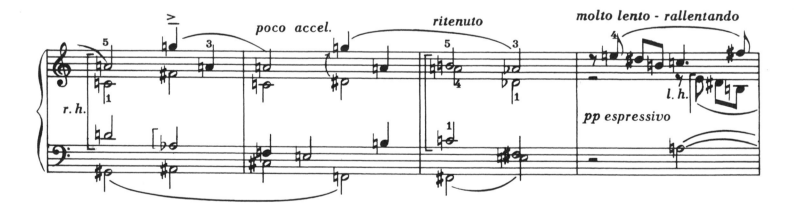